THE POEM SHE DIDN'T WRITE AND OTHER POEMS

ALSO BY OLENA KALYTIAK DAVIS

On the Kitchen Table from Which Everything Has Been Hastily Removed (chapbook)

shattered sonnets love cards and other off and back handed importunities

And Her Soul out of Nothing

OLENA KALYTIAK DAVIS

COPPER CANYON PRESS
PORT TOWNSEND, WASHINGTON

Printed in the United States of America

Cover design by Phil Kovacevich

Copper Canyon Press is in residence at Fort Worden State Park in Port Townsend, Washington, under the auspices of Centrum. Centrum is a gathering place for artists and creative thinkers from around the world, students of all ages and backgrounds, and audiences seeking extraordinary cultural enrichment.

LIBRARY OF CONGRESS CATALOGING-IN-PUBLICATION DATA

Davis, Olena Kalytiak.
[Poems. Selections]
The Poem she didn't write and other poems / Olena Kalytiak Davis.
pages cm
ISBN 978-1-55659-459-5 (hardback)
I. Title.
PS3554.A93757A6 2014
811'.54—dc23

2014018142

98765432 FIRST PRINTING

Copper Canyon Press
Post Office Box 271
Port Townsend, Washington 98368
www.coppercanyonpress.org

ACKNOWLEDGMENTS/ENCOMIUM/DEDICATION

thanks to all who
helped write (Foundations: Guggenheim! and Rasmuson!)
and publish these poems,
which, unlike everything else i ever and always and
endlessly do, are actually NOT
for gobi and lyana,

(ENCOMIUM

On the one hand, long-legged JOY,
dressed in a tutu, leopard-print leggings,
and a "top model" tank, turning
landing a cartwheel finished
all of her homework at school!

On the other, long-haired INTELLIGENCE
AND COMPASSION, all hoodied up,
puffy sneakers, a backpack heavy with ichthyology
texts, composing an opposition to Milton
on marital dissolution, thoughtful, so, a bit
slow-

O mine, fairer and more incorruptible!
Saviors of Lacedaemon and Hellas!
Their beautiful and blooming faces!

SQUINKY-SQUINKY!
SQUINKY-SQUINKY!

My immortality on a skateboard!)

but, of course and again, (unknown) "Reader, for you."

I love you. All your concerns are as important to me as my own. For many dear, beautiful reasons I wish to make you happy.

CONTENTS

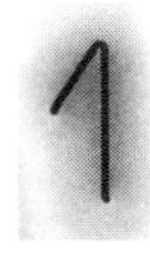

2

THE POEM SHE DIDN'T WRITE AND OTHER POEMS

1

Summer Fiction

My fancies fluttered round the same images
like martins round a bell tower at dawn.
I checked my e-mails, then, I checked them again:
lariat sweep and stallion glow.
Some one hour's experience for which we
stubbornly subornatively return:
a dalliance at an execution.
Everything reduced to occasion

but the dailiness of my great Slavic beauty,
unwitnessed, being passed on and through. But

green after green after green!
Summer like summer like summer!
Fat, like Tolstoy's—
inside the house and out, fat!
Gathering raspberries in a bikini (*chto takoe?*)
as if the will of everyman were free!

The great Sky over Austerlitz.
The old Oak near Otradnoe.
The Hut at Mytishchi.
The Platform at Astapovo Station.

In the Backyard in a Billabong Bikini.

Each day you did not see me was something
you lost, like, at cards.

After Grass and Long Knives

Suspect enthusiasm—
having eaten pins before—
but that's what keeps one
quiet, that's what makes one

stay. Empty is just the first
temporal name
after something smaller sat there is gone.

Then that space
regains its height and wild.

Let let lovers be
light thoughts, just touch
remembered in some not unkind way.

It was all fine.
It was all right.

And now what's next is
clerestory:

wait become place—and not a cowardly one—
like in some great house made of purest plank,
place to pause, place to be welcomed.

The Lyric "I" Drives to Pick Up Her Children from School: A Poem in the Postconfessional Mode

"i" has not found, started, finished "i's" morning poem,
the poem "i" was writing about "i" having sex with the man "i" left her
husband for
the night before or maybe just this morning.
a sex poem, so to speak, so to say, so as to lay...
a foundation for...
what????????

SEX

i lost my sex/poem!
how did it go?
i know it was called

SEX

something about my bosky acres,
my unshrubb'd down
'bout all being tight and yare

(bring in tiresias?)
did you say soothe?
tiresias, who lies fucking more?
whoops.

~~who~~ likes ~~fucking more~~?

("bring in // the old thought // [allen grossman doing yeats]
that life prepares us for // what never happens")

today (~~the color of~~) my sex
was lavender then yellow
gold then muted mossy grey and green

i bid my lover
lower
i bid my lover shhhhhhh

i bid my lover
linger

i bid my
lover, go

~~*lover, go!*~~
~~*(see!)*~~

i bid my lover stay
away

"i" notices it is almost time to pick up her children from school!
"i" realizes she has gotten nowhere, nowhere near it, much less inside it, wasted another morning, can't fucking write a poem to save "i's" life, oh well,
"i" is, at least, "working".
"i" pulls on her tight jeans, her big boots, her puffy parka.
"i" remote-starts her car.
"i's" car is a 1995 red toyota 4-runner with racing stripe that doesn't have enough power for "i".
"i's" car stereo also doesn't have enough power for "i".
"i" drives cross town listening to dylan, who has plenty of power for "i".
"i" wonders how why dylan isn't "i's" man.
"i" gets some looks from some lesser men, some in better, more powerful trucks, even though "i's" dirty dirty-blonde hair is covered by a woolen cap.
"i" feels the power of being a single mom in a red truck.
"i" knows it is not enough power.
"i" thinks "i am the man, i suffered, i was there".
"i" is almost broke, but
"i" thinks "i live more in a continuous present that i enjoy".
"i" thinks "amor fati".

"i" notices the chugach mountains.
"i" notices the chugach mountains sometimes look good and sometimes bad.
"i" remembers that yesterday the chugach mountains looked desolate and dirty and roadblocky.
"i" notices the chugach mountains look particularly beautiful today covered in sun and snow.
"i" almost thinks "bathed in sun and snow" but stops herself.
"i" feels that "i" can maybe find, really start, really finish her sex poem tomorrow.
"i" likes the dubus thing about adultery having a morality of its own.
"i" also likes "human drama".
"i" really enjoyed "i ♥ huckabees".
"i" thought sex was overrated for a long time, then not for a year and a half, and now, again.
"i" gives, well, has given, good head.
"i" takes it like a man.
"i" thinks there should be a new "new sexualized and radicalized poetry of the self",
"i" knows the "single-minded frenzy of a raving madman" but,
"i" mostly keeps her head.
"i" remembers that "as long ago as 1925, boris tomashevsky, a leading russian formalist critic, observed that the 'autobiographical poem' is one that mythologizes the poet's life in accordance with the conventions of his time. it relates not what has occurred but what should have occurred, presenting an idealized image of the poet as representative of his literary school".
"i" wants to be a man like marjorie perloff, helen hennessy vendler, boris tomashevsky.
"i" thinks, on the other hand, "i mean i like in art when the artist doesn't know what he knows in general; he only knows what he knows specifically".
"i" thinks: "that mantel piece is clean enough or my name isn't bob rauschenberg".
"i" just wishes "i" could talk more smarter theory, no
"i" just wishes "i" could write more smarter poems, no

"i" thinks "WHY I AM A POET AND NOT A..."
"i" thinks "KALYTIAK DAVIS PAINTS A PICTURE".
"i" wants to include the word *coruscate* in it, and, possibly, a quote from
rudolf steiner.
"i" wishes she could remember abrams's definition of the structure of the greater romantic lyric, but that it presents "a determinate speaker in a particularized, and usually localized, outdoor setting, whom we overhear as he carries on, in a fluent vernacular which rises easily to a more formal speech, a sustained colloquy, sometimes with himself or with the outer scene, but more frequently with a silent human auditor, present or absent" and that "the speaker begins with a description of the landscape" and that "an aspect or change of aspect in the landscape evokes a varied but integral process of memory, thought, anticipation, and feeling which remains closely intervolved with the outer scene" and that "in the course of this meditation the lyric speaker achieves an insight, faces up to a tragic loss, comes to a moral decision, or resolves an emotional problem" and that "often the poem rounds upon itself to end where it began, at the outer scene, but with an altered mood and deepened understanding which is the result of the intervening meditation" evades her.
"i" wants to say "silent human auditor, are you absent or present?" but
"i" knows "i" makes, has made, that move too often.
"i" knows "i" is alone in her red truck.
"i" reconsiders, perhaps it is like giving good head?
"i" thinks *his his he himself,* but not too bitterly, then
"i" thinks "i", then,
"i" thinks "you".
"i" has not told her lover that "i" is not in love with him any longer, but
"i" knows he knows, must know.
"i" has not told her lover that "i" had a long conversation with "i's"
x-husband on the phone last night.
"i" thinks "my sidestepping and obliquities".
"i" thinks love is what went wrong.
"i" feels elizabeth bishop reprimanding "i".

"i" thinks like a gentle loving firm almost slap but really just a squeeze of, not on, the hand from a, the, mother neither one of them had for very long, long enough.
"i" has not thought of "i's" dead mother in a long time.
"i" thinks of jonathan letham and his dead mother and his wall of books.
"i" thinks of mark reagan and his walls and walls of books, and how his landlord, fearing collapse, made him move to the bottom floor.
"i" thinks of doug teter and his smaller, but still, wall of books.
"i" thinks of jude law.
"i" thinks jude law probably doesn't know how to read.
"i" knows that no lover can be her "objective correlative", still
"i" thinks "so true a lover as theagenes".
"i" thinks "so constant a friend as pylades".
"i" thinks "so valiant a man as orlando".
"i" thinks "so right a prince as xenophon's cyrus".
"i" thinks "so excellent a man in every way as virgil's aeneas".
"i" notices dylan is almost done singing "to ramona".
"i" loves "everything passes, everything changes, just do what you think you should do".
"i" thinks dylan is singing to "i".
"i" thinks he means now, and now, and now; daily.
"i" is almost there.
"i" wonders if "i's" meditation is too long, has gotten away from "i".
"i" thinks it should take precisely as long as the ride: 15 minutes tops; well, 30 in a snowstorm.
"i" knows it is not snowing.
"i" wonders if "i" should at this point even refer to "i's" meditation.
"i" thinks "man can embody truth but he cannot know it".
"i" thinks "especially under stress of psychological crisis".
"i" thinks what's worse, anaphora or anaphrodesia?
"i" thinks of the diaphragm still inside her.
"i" shudders at the audacity of her sex.
"i" is exactly on time to pick up her daughter.
"i" must wait another 45 minutes to retrieve her son.

"i" will try and remember to remove it promptly when they get back to "i's" house, i.e., home.

"i" has fucked with the facts so "you" think she's robert lowell. (*but whoever saw a girl like robert lowell?*)

"i" doesn't care if "you", silent human auditor, present or absent, never heard of, could give a flying fuck about, robert lowell.

Robert Lowell

The dream, I don't remember how it went,
For I don't really dream or count or know
Why Robert Lowell: the only poet shade sent
To acknowledge my cool ambition, light my cigarette.

This is the decade of aughts and oughts
And I am still naught. I am forty. In a tight
T-shirt over my small ignoble breasts reading:
"ALL'S MISALLIANCE". Downward woman,

Upward fish, said to him: What is it that you wish?
Sir, on a brackish reach of shoal, is that
Where we first met? I want to say it is
But however impressive rhetoric that...

It wouldn't be "true". I **am** a fraction more,
Though, Sir, much much less than you. I
Know how to change neither myself nor
Earth nor sky. I don't even try. Sailor,

Cousin, Cal, though I am dark and against
The grain, I don't do what I do and I am
Not plain. And though I stare I can't see
My face. Or hands. Or hair. Lowell: *In a nother*

Ten years' dream path life I would have fallen
Heels over your pretty hellish head,
I would have asked, and what would you have said?
Said? Without vision how can I improvise?

Without imprimatur how can I mature?
Without ground, how can I grind (the cool-
Ing grindstone of **whose** ambition?), how can I stand?
Said: Sir, Sad. I still breathe the ether of my first

Marriage feast and, man, it's bad. I am full-famished.
Famished-full. Breed? Idiot up, pedant down,
And that there rag, that's my wedding gown. Not to mention
Incest, parricide, Sir, miscegenation...

Naked in my raincoat, singing up my
Second rate, I wake now to find myself
This long this late. This low. Alone. *If poisonous*
Minerals, and if that tree... Which part is dream

And which part life? Which part poet which part
Wife? Which parts his, theirs, and which part wholly
Mine? I see. I steal. Where is the part of bringing it
Back to what you (i mean I!) really feel? Why, Mr. Robert

Lowell, why do we dream count marry die? Who strewed
These flowers at my feet, and will he be back
To make it nice and neat? Green and doomed,
When will I finally learn how and when to leave a room?

If lecherous goats... and *if serpents envious...*
MY GOD WHERE IS MOTHERFUCKING YOURS, HIS,
MINE, OURS, MERCY BEING EASY, AND GLORIOUS?

no, i would have said: *No.* sorry, sir, but i'm
the kind that dare dispute with thee as you/
i do with me. i hope you don't mind.

i don't know how to have and hold. keep what?
keep where? i lose and fold. unable to make
or mark (or count) as i am taught and told,
i must re-lay, re-do, re-dound, re-doubt.

I will not marry.

hey grey and grizzled sir, does this one count?
or was it just in/for fun? oh well, who cares,
i'm done. at least i think i'm don(n)e. no,

I will go on, and this is how it went:
O, said Mr. Robert Lowell, *though sand, (you, you are,)*
My Dear, you are a lovely piece of land.

The Late Repentant (Antepurgatory)

it took dante and virgil
it took lowell on dante and eliot and eliot on...
all the men were drinking, well-educated, and speaking all at once
(to this horrible music
i learned to ______ your _____)

even in paradise they wait for their bodies

i'm incorporeal
when you're (___) near

SONNET (stopped)

hey baby—good morning/evening/morrow/night—
i awoke to burning wet purple leaves
and a wet roof blue light. you are not here—
but you are somewhere—in your t-shirt: tight and bright.

count, note, these rhymed lines that do not
break. count
on me i'll come around again: like clockwork:
every twenty minutes: stop and stop.
like this, again and again; again! take

me, never give (me) up. we are each's
other: the ultimate double entendre and
someday these words will still be lit on fire
in some tattered book washed up upon some beach.

don't ask the cost; (for now) i give this shit for free:
i live to give you more than you give me.

Complaint

would that i could
have a lover
that should write a sonnet
on over
me

it might start on a lark
in the light of the dark
at the top of my crown
and end in a couplet at my feet

the rhyme would be fine there
would be no line unnecessary
or covered in dust

'twould finally prove that i am
as fine and fit as a clam
worthy of great love and much lust

'stead said he (and i para-
phrase) something like this:

she goes like a ship
through my thin and my thick
leaving no shoal left unexplored or unlicked
she flames and she flickers
never bites never bickers
whether to attend to the lee or the aft
her red lips do insist
to kiss me to bliss
long and strong are her grenadier arms
whether lank and loose at her sides
(and lord, her midriff **is** *toned*
in accord with the Times
the new erogenous zone)

or tight round my then bejeweled and embraced neck
she's bedecked with features so fine
dark as soot are her eyes
halibut white are her thighs
gold and untame as a cat's is her mane
and methinks her lynx soft wild meek and insane
her nose squarely and boldly reposes,
in her cheeks i find meadow-pink roses and wink, wink,
her rump is quite plump to boot
though her teats are too small
really that's all
that my lady lacks in the dawn or the dusk
but whether clad or undressed
her love she doth not profess
ah well, there's a certain rapport with the dirth
which all the more
leaves room for a haven...

oh low
flush
lush
shallow
slow
heaven
unleavening
this
huge
round
horrible
horny
earth

but 'twas not good enough for my ear nor my need
so i sent him away with no other in stead

Late-Night Poemcall

flatfish comma question mark,
hello?

after not seeing "him" for "so-long!"
a time...

a bald friend
in a dream
in a hat

not sure

"what"
"that"
"meant"

we were looking out for coppers
who were in turn
looking out for

"love"
end-stopped—

at the corner of 5th and "SEE"

"i" mean "i" mean
dean and "i" and
dean stopped "writing"
years ago

last "said" he:
my,
what pretty "legs" you have,
"poem"

bitterly?

yeanling augie says
or will or would say,
swimmingly:
kinda like-a flipbook, mama, no?

solon says:
windfall
counts, go...

being hatted for so long...

did you say "hated"?
no.

being hatted for so long...

did you say "mated"?
no.

i said "matted",
oh—

now, done
now, gone
now, more

so-long-as
a scarf
is a lost friend
in the end

yes dean; yes, dean,
yestreen i saw...

mary ruefle endued in a leopardskinpillboxhat

was that mary ruefle?

or being “fat” with,
having been,
and then “some”

lean in, love,

that *was* mary ruefle!

as slinky
as a slinky

or a spirograph

wow
now

let’s “practice”
our “craft”

let’s practice
our math:

ten yen
minus ten yen
“equals”

augie aptly questioneth:
what about the classical unities
of place
and time?

and inside my bedroom
mushroomed
a longleaf pine

if you want me to "yearn"
leave "now"
leave "town"
leave years gaps gasps between
(just) leave

a "dirty" message on my "machine"

so much the better to "_____ you" with...

o sweet floccose!

"down" is just as good
a word

to put down
to go down on

o "down" covered and "dawn" colored
poem!

oh, "come on"
i'm just "____ing" with you...

why so agape
at my agape?

it's a platonic
tonic

did you say "chthonic"?

no.

leave "unseen"

a green pen/sharp(ie) i think it was, mark
on your
"jeans"

i forgot
you were that “tall”!

meet me
at flattop?

no.

second circle?

F train?

oh!

and then,
“sex”
again.

the contract i signed
said sang “nothing” “about” “under”
the lids of my eyes

every day
could be like this, no?

yes and.
yes and.

okay, let’s regroup

(no.)

let’s all be alone
in the same “room”

kalyootsoos,
let’s have a meeting

“about love”

o courtiers
soldiers
scholars
poets
patrons
friends

prithee

if you “want” me

to “learn”

“tell” me:

are “we”?

please,

i beg of you,

o.

Cho(o)se Love

i did not look to love,
but looking loving moved

(or maybe all i did was look?)

i did not look to fuck,
but looking fucking moved

and moved

and fucking moved
and moved

i did not choose to lose
but choosing loomed
and rose

and momentarily
something in me unfroze

moved, i made my move

i moved my new address: i live alone
with my twigborers and wanderoos

come visit, love,

a new dress, worn for
torn by

you

left carried out
carried through

left
right?

chose love
chose "you"

chose love
chose true

chose love?
chose true?

excuse me, but,
fuck you

what oh what can i say?
that i have sat on that shelf called wife, called self, called duty, called
    fooled, called fool,
hopped off chanting: choose love, choose love, choose

love

choose true

friends, romans, excuse me, pardon me, no, not you, rommie,
    countrymen, lend me a precise and proportioning ear: hopped off,
    bent over, chose
love

interpret as you will
had no ill will
thought was welling what hurt

was so willing
bent over (again and again)
for love

they say: to her heart's content
her heart's content
was blood and goo

cogent, wild, and blue

and/but moved right on
on by
on through

'twas it only adultery with a flute player?
or was it just the flute?
(maybe all i did was fuck...)

a fluke, an open flue
you you you

the pronoun
that refuses to attach
to anyone or thing
whether tried
or tired or new or old or true

even if you know his hair color
his eyes
his "you"

yours truly

false or true?

j'accuse je m'accuse je am a recluse
recklessandlostandloose
and here's my noose:
thought i thought i thought
it through

i stand i sit i lie
alone
accused

fou

c'est ça

excuse me?

c'est ça!

c'est la
roving eye and hand and thigh

yeux main gigot

c'est what?

fuck you! i say sa: thought and thought
and thought i thought it through
chose love chose true

gauche
droit?

i did not rove to love
(but i did love to rove...)

i did not look to lick
i did not lick to trick
i did not...
sorry love, thought i
thought i thought i

choix droit
choisi vrai
choisi true

and naked and plain and honest and simple

and sober and exact and straight and god's and absolute and intrinsic and
 hard and stern
and gospel and bible and whole
and nothing but...

vous!

right on!
write on...

whatever you write on
you will never be right
and the way it will read

in your biography will be auto
matic and mantic and mastic
auto accurate and actual and factual and verified and certified and sooth
and true

and strong and long and wrong.
and dull
and due

it should be short
just a shot
a shoot
a volume or two:

it should just say: tried tasted chewed
meretricious love

connubial, too

say it:
thought
i thought i thought
it through

so someday, they will read it
on your tombstone, if they can part
the long leaves of grass, for you have been
engraving it daily
using the wrongest and bluntest of tools
it will be cracked and pounded and blundered and beaten
in and out and through:
hey, before i lied and lay
down here, naked and alone and tired and sad and, good lord, good and dead:

loved

tried

choosing

loving

you

Threshold

unWELCOMEd
he stepped
into my HOUSE

past (,) the photos on the refrigerator
past (,) my children
past (,) my well-appointed LIFE

Not This

my god all the days we have lived thru
saying

not this
one, not this,
not now,
not yet, this week
doesn't count, was lost, this month
was shit, what a year, it sucked,
it flew, that decade was for
what? i raised my kids, they
grew i lost two pasts—i am
not made of them and they
are through.

we forget what
we remember:

each of the five
the fevered few

days we used
to fall in love.

I Had a Ski-Masked Rapist in My House

no, i'm not kidding (you). no, i am not
mad (at him). no. that motherfucker wrestled me
down (like a motherfucking angel)
zip-tied my motherfucking wrists to the black
motherfucking headboard (all motherfucking
behind my back) motherfucker handled me
(violently) no (gently) no he was confused yes
motherfucker, yes, motherfucking (un)hand(ed) me

the rest
of my (beautiful and true)
motherfucking life.

Commentary

depends on the day; today:
the first show/snow of march.
we are proceeding
from winter to winterstill the windowsill
thick with icicles/gnarled spindly geraniums ancient
in human years. the soft
cat in her soft bed. the hard
hip at the hard (kitchen) counter, as always, all
stay and delay and nothing, and sometimes, just
nothingyet, and timesother:
nothingfuckingever.
nothingfuckingmore

(fuckingnoonenewnow)
(fuckingnoonenew!)

sat this
morning that
poem came
walking by. said: pup,
get back to breathing. said: shut up
and write this down:

it must be more spectacular in its absence!

(*you* must be more spectacular in your absence...)

mind strayed. i stayed
till the alarm went off. there is a hole
in the tree outside the (bedroom) window—into
which i sometimes
looks. aftertimes i finds: it is not

a hole
at all.

Lime Tree Bower

i stood and sat and somehow
knew or thought to thank
the VIOLENCELIKELIGHT
i did not call upon in the dark

i'm better for it

SONNET (silenced)

with her unearned admixable beauty
she sat up on the porch and asked for (f)light;
answerable only to poetry—
and love—to make it thru the greyblue night

blew smoke into words and even whiter ghosts
that could see what others in this broad dark
could not: she set to make of nothing most,
better: an everenlightening mark:

ghost gave her this: a piece of flint: that if
you rubbed the right way,
the lightlessness would come down, give up, lift—
and then there would be nothing left to say.

o sterilize the lyricism of
my sentence: make me plain again my love

(my ghost)
(and dumb)

Fragmentary

no elaborate rhetorical structure
this poem
is no pawn
is just a little game
horses jumping night intact
gerhard richter for some reason appears
the paint
digital and smeared
taint

Kafka and Milena About to Meet in Vienna

when i first met you i had a dream
that exactly what happened happened

when i first met you i thought
"what would i think if i already knew you"

when i first met you
you were a stiff applicant

you were wearing a ski mask
you told me you could hurt me
you zip-tied my wrists to the headboard
you duct-taped my mouth
you said you would not hurt me
you tore off my pants

you said:
i never get to say your name
(your name your name)

when i last saw you
i absently kissed you; i was kinda late for a plane

when i last saw you
i handed you a poem in which you were already dead

when i last saw you
you misunderstood what i hadn't yet just said

when i last saw you
there was a blanket over my head
you said you knew where i lived

the threshold and the backward glance
i am glad you aren't here now

but (in the margins) i am also sad

not your face

only the way you walked away
through the tables in the café

your figure, your dress

Threshold

your (foot)
    fall

your (foot)
    fault

  the
     sweating

     urn

  the sandal
  with a broken

     strap
       (*you know what that's for*)

my reluctance is, i can assure you, coequal with your
dismay

Alaska Aubade (Winter)

the longest night—the selfsame dark—
you know it well, the descent that both begins and ends
in lark, in nightingale, in hell—bleaker depths
reserved for crows way better (less wide) than you:

saying (to yourself): you will ride this still-dark out
and you will go on to tell the other birds about
the not even so urgent falling upon oneself
because one's lover is not (t)here.

you chose so well! so hot
on the other side of the equator!

you know best how to touch
yourself and treat you bad.
if you sleep long enough there will be light,
the bed will be empty and be right, longing,

kafka's, to your right, the stack of books—ha,
one written by your latest lover.
bass upon my trespass, dear—
his photo on the back cover.

he told me the sky was yellow over where he lied.
it was orange here for just a moment.
the sky, all that's left
of your choughed and chewed, your
humanity.

oh, no one's fucking anyone black-and-blue
the world has no color 'cept that we imbue
will will eventually be enough
be 'clept life: half-lit half-lived

loved by half, alas they thought you titillating and sad
o so dirty sexy.

the sex and the poetry—weren't they supposed to be
bigger and better than this? than fucking me?

The Poem She Didn't Write

began
when she stopped

began in winter and, like everything else, at first, just waited for spring
in spring noticed there were lilac branches, but no desire,
no need to talk to any angel, to say: sky, dooryard, ______,
when summer arrived there was more, but not much
nothing really worth noting
and then it was winter again—nothing had changed: sky, dooryard,
_______, white, frozen was the lake and the lagoon, some froze the ocean
(*now you erase that*) (*you cross that out*)
and so on and so forth
didn't want
didn't want to point, to catalogue, to inquire,
to acknowledge, to uncover, not even to transcend
wasn't ambitious, wasn't ambiguous, wasn't
____-reflexive, ____-referential,
the "poet-narrator" did not "want to be liked"
got even stronger: no longer wanted
"to be"
until "wasn't"
was what was missing
was enough

the paper need not (was) not
function(ing) as air (*please stop*) (*please shut the fuck up*)

THE POEM SHE DIDN'T WRITE

had no synecdoches, no metonymy, no pattern, if it rhymed—it was
purely accidental,
no non sequitur, no primogenitor, wasn't
influenced by homer or blake or yeats   auden   contained
no anxiety, hadn't even heard of
louise glück franz wright billy (budd?) collins

(in the margin: "*then why are you so sad?*")

spring summer fall
and so on and so forth
it was and it was and it was

done

she did not read it to anyone
she did not send it out "for publication"   when asked
she said she "was not writing" because
"she wasn't"

          But somehow   (like a rumor)

                    THE POEM

SHE DIDN'T WRITE got out   maybe
she talked about it in her sleep   maybe
she was betrayed by a lover

(and in the margin: "*and why are you so sad?*")

In   THE POEM SHE DIDN'T WRITE
there was nothing poetic.
In   THE POEM
there were no hidden references to ____________.
In   THE POEMSHEDIDN'TWRITE
arthur rimbaud was not a hero.
In   THEPOEMSHEDIDN'TWRITE
people did not turn to each other in mania or desperation   preservation
In   THEPOEM
away in boredom   disappointment   despair

                    THE POEM

was equally hailed and dismissed by the critics.
harold bloom said: "otherness to such a degree that loneliness was created and alleviated at once".
helen vendler wrote: "a posthumous consciousness imputed to the poet's corpse; a hoped-for future represented as though it has already happened".
___________: "the marriage of marivaux and poussin, i.e., poussinesque maurivaudage"
: "an anti-master floribund disaster"
: "fawn meets wolf"
: "exudes sexuality like a dark french perfume"

poets turned in their tombs
hopkins's skull shifted   nothing could be counted   was this finally S=P=R=U=N=G rhythm?
there was hysteria and histrionic personality   disorder   low affect aphonia   apophasis   andyet
THE POEM
(people need(ed) shorthand and so the rest of the title began to be elided) was   some how   able to act
some said   THE POEM

"could not exist, because it, um, didn't"
some said "it existed only in that space between 'out there' and 'in here'   catullus's   mistress's   sandaled foot stepping/suspended over the threshold
some exegesised that "rilke had already not written it"
some opined that like all the other poems—it only didn't exist in academia, if it didn't exist at all
i.e., somewhere in a park near athens "duh", said some, "ever heard of derrida? as the poet need not be present then why present the poem?"
some said its presence   as with all poetry   written or not was "contingent

on a reader (or non-
reader, as the case may be) and only if that reader bent over it late at night
called it 'beloved'"

others agreed because now they could quote some stevens: "yes, yes, they said,
late and leaning"

others maintained that it SO didn't matter, they would go on the way they had been doing and their parents before them and their parents' parents
(a cat's flux)

: "tries, but fails, to cross over into different worlds"
: "not worthy of my love"
: "an assassination at an assignation"
: "(nothing is(n't) real, everything is(n't) possible)"

but the lilacs, the lilacs
blooming, blooming   (on) (in) winter

i.e., nothing had changed   and yet   and   none
the   less: a new world order
the point had been made: things that didn't exist   existed more
existed ever   existed over... (*watchit!*)
("*because complexity never made anyone feel better")
she had given them permission (not) to   proceed
soon   hopefully   other writers would stop

(writing(;))
THEPOEM

was some body's thesis and some body's else's dumbest joke
it made literary terms like ______ and ________ obsolete
it made literary theories like ________ and _________ sound stupider than ever

in the 22nd century they would talk about "she" being hit with a "fish"
they would confuse "she" with all the great poets who really weren't so good, were they?
(all small and flawed men)
five hundred years later a fragment would be found a fragment
that also couldn't didn't
exist
and so forth and so on on in

lilacs on in
winters

THEPOEM

was repeatedly misattributed it crossed and re-crossed
genres
some said it had once been a charlie kaufman movie or
a novel by davidfosterwallace
was it rauschenberg or was it dekooning?
who erased whom?

what?

it was the ascension and the ceiling and the sonnets except
better 'cause refused to be
refused to participate in a world made up of and by ants and
dogs and armadillos peacocks skunks
(ref. swarthmore chart)

my name is verdant greene.

i am the HUNTER GRACCHUS.

call me.........

BUT by now (then)   every   one   was   dead

but for now,

in the year of
THEPOEM
20__
finally:

a poetry the masses could rally around—
"so simple" they intoned "and yet so brilliant"
people began crossing poetry off the list of what they, too, disliked
someone began carrying a sign, as if it was a demonstration: "CLEAR YOUR MIND OF CANT" someone else copied it but added an apostrophe
splinter groups became political (INSERT SOMETHING HERE ON KANT) (*the starry skies above me and the moral law inside me*?)
"why didn't the poets invent it sooner?" they bemusedly wondered
(smelling their faux lilac boutonnieres)
slightly giddy with relief they became a little careless and self-aggrandizing
"why didn't WE think of it?"
"my six-year-old could have done it!"
"how did we live (not) not thinking about poetry, when, after all, that was all there ever wasn't".

2

Fragmentary

poem after
poem after
something after someone

why do you just want more, more, more
more, more, more, more, more?

the person in the poem's loud silence
waiting for the band to come back on

SONNET (falling objects)

and then some of us souls, john self, nam le
piccarda donati, caduta massi,
maybe me, stood around and shot the shit:
why were we all here? by whose scary wit

were we written into this italian script?   text?
con- what? what now? who with whom? what next?

chiusa chiusa
canto
canta
canti

(how far to be beloved?
to be believed?)

(And More)

(o (l)uxu/orious (p)/(l)ussuria) one can rule rimini
and still not rule (or rim) me. doric, ionic, phallic: i
liked it all. i moaned and wept as i do now, but it
was a joy and a different kind of sorrow:
to see your lover's eyes when he's down there. down there
the very root *was* the very root, and fig was fruit and nut
gelato. down here how it happened can still make me shudder.
sigh.
just how far down, sinner, must you go? whatever pleases you:
follow my tail, my thigh. and: VIDE FICA MIA. eat my furbelowed
heart, tremble at my furbo and my body gone but still beautiful
heart, this life that's for the birds is saved by rhyming such as our
heart, if you twist my arm just right i'll loose my mind.

the new style is the old style: from behind.

SONNET (motion)

i saw you spin: pause once pause twice pause t(h)rice;
too fast you went for me to catch my love,
from that from then was dizzy as a dove
dipping low as sister hawk after (her) mice.

heads up! head down to draw upon that straw:
i'm sorry, love, these teeth were in my mouth
before we met before i knew that south
could be as warm as italy or dawn.

right now. who needs prepare to subjugate?!
i give you my self-portrait: you say: look:
it's fawn meets wolf. it's sex meets book.
it's love, love, it's all, it's not too late:

then push and pull took on "self loved self-hate":
dead on. my god. i won. you fucked me straight.

Francesca Says More

that maiden thump *was* book on floor, but
does it really matter who kissed who
first or then who decided to go further?
lower? faster? naturally, we took
turns on top. *now here, now there, and up*
and down... once it started no one even thought to think to stop.
so, we have holes inside our souls,
but mustn't we begin by filling others'?
god gave us lips and hands and parts
that cannot possibly be saved for prayer. nor by.
i will not name name, claim fame by how well
or who i fucked or why, it happens all the time.
and it's you, white pilgrim, whom next galehot seeks.

fuck. we didn't read again for weeks.

"House" Is Being Cleared

house is forever—being cleaned—
the children hate to watch it go—
every scrap to them is treasure
loss found the second time—anew

house is forever being—cleared—
to help me decide—who—
i make high heaps of harbored stuff
then watch the rick fall—through—

collide with floor—strike the board—
"less fell" i make into our daily bread—
then again i wait until
i can heap store speak—again

house is—forever being moored
to unmoorish moony things—
like springs from toys—
and spring—

pestilence too—i thought i liked
my poisons in pretty little cups—
but the mouses in my closet
have put me on—the cusp—

house unhoused itself this morn—
the way it does when i like that do sing—
beneath the fingers of a man—
i didn't quite ask—in

house refused to sail away
it stayed with me—within—
together we used the windows
to count macaws—and sin—

house is settled—mine—
he's learned to send himself—away—
knock later if you must, you will—persist—now
empty only looks and sounds—to the amateur—amiss—

Fragmentary

alison mosshart in this poem
jack white is in this poem
kurt vile is in this poem
meta-poetry dude black pants hair
the way the head bangs the drum
this way this way yeah
that's good

Just Now

and another endless (seemedlong! seemedless!) seamless summer
froze slowly suddenly stubbornly
into the longshoredandmetered longandserious winter
i would skate on it
savor my wavering
before choosing a firmer stance
stand of misery or trees
a firmament for my little bees
'twas when they were all in love with me
and "me" was just aborning

not that i (k)new it
not that i (k)now it

but this just now is
the time i would look back
later on as sublime
hook and eye: was blonde
and young at 41
i loved my life my sex
though i was no longer in love
with my lover and thus,
this, from the mouth
of a Ukrainian mother

Alaska Aubade (Summer)

although 'twas very late when someone took
the truth and dared to touch what untouched
belonged only to another

o teeth and flash
once skinflint sun fingered
the summer flesh of the unfamiliar

thigh wellmet thigh and sigh
sent sigh searching for what yet could be
uncovered: (o to die into this life

this light)

the truth took time
night never fell and now and still
the willow cleanly crying in the window

that refused the lullaby abides
unmet unsatisfied *stay*
atop the white white covers
more and so much (endless) light by which to see

your lover

Sight Unseen

you are. but see(n) in me? you?
gulled by blonde confusion? know(n):
i'm a pretty face with just one pretty eye.
my self-worth what? its weight in storm.

too soon the moon was high and full
a "beautiful and serious" boy from "the tower" went
and i by old ghosts and ugly witches sent to bring you—
what? a self of heavy sinew and unrectored chaos made?

"come here!" you innocently (it is a fairy tale) said
and licked those lips all mortal women like (to kiss), no, love—

i(t) skipped a beat, or two, i(t) tripped some steps
listened to a lot of songs, read a short story, ran a mile, seven, twenty,
smoked a cigarette a joint a pipe a pack vermont new york seattle back—
a prestidigitation of the heart. what? i(t) turned around and came—

fleet, her winged feet,
black, the color of her true love's hair.

SONNET (division)

fuck! i have two loves too, i really do:
my one is blonde, my other's hair is black,
but neither either vice nor virtue lacks
and each complete to me is fair(e) and true.

i have not held them side to side, nor wished
as with less(er) love(s) to have them: back to back.
if evil choose a place to lay its wrack
it lie(s) with "i": that stenched and (w)retched dish

(i has not seen me as they must) of self,
and if me looks i can but lose. suggest me!
take me! then back to unalike give me:
to husband, wife, then back upon my shelf:

here (this) my wicked rest: i scribes this text.
"i" blithely rhymed: fuck! all... is aural sex.

To an Italian Ceiling

all my life, that year, they tried to take my soul from me.
and not like i had a soul,
and not like it was such a prize—

but at least i(t) was black-lunged and thumbed.
although ornate, you are high and flat; untouched,
untouchable, and dumb.

it went on the way i do: alone.
let a ski-masked rapist into my home.
and even in that moment was at least
two.

it's true: i want to leave.
but i do not want to leave
you.

maybe i have lost my lover
in my wisdom and his error
i know i have cost my lover
euros of late summer grief

but i was briefly what he wanted
beatrice in an overgroomed italian garden
in bvulgari sunglasses and thigh-high boots

all was roses and pomegranates, persimmons
o the pearlike sweetness, the ache
the muscatel, the grapes
in this particular heaven.

what went wrong was nothing, is (that i fell from) this:
can someone please
take a look at the wet dark

illumined union
in the italian bathtub
look how
the voice continues reading
as all of italy goes dark

in all too brief relief
his wisdom and my error
a thirty years' body and a six o'clock face
that i am finally for once
the one still
listening
the italian alps to shadow
the text to wet lace.

Mean and Manly and Meant

i was glad you called
although i had not been thinking about you
at all.

hadn't given it a second
thought
neither carried nor brought
no face to mind

or at least, not yours, when i tried
again and again to come

do you know how many men would paykilldie
for me to suck their cock? *fuck.*

this is how i am: more
horace than catullus: just plain mean
and manly
and meant.

Fragmentary

o fucking poem
not you again
showing off your tight your tan
how old are you anyway?
gena rowlands in this one
fake drunk on opening night
very very very fakedrunk

Francesca Says Too Much

each day i came an infinity of times; it rained and reign
was so complete with every pleasure as if in love i sang.
pity you're confused: 'twasn't love. it was sex that dissolved me:
limo **was** body and mud. and long and shiny
and briny what i polished with my tongue marmo hard and pallina
smooth once whetted i never stopped saying sipa, was always in
position, in the mood, too much was never enough. i kept open
my arms my legs my eyes my lips moving lifted to heaven
my ass my hips. pilgrim, can you picture it? my tits. and it was
all wet. don't cry. dry your ablutionary tears. no thing now can absolve me:
but i regret it not: i was so alive! o, to again have
someone's occhi and fingers and penes on in me, to be
licked and sucked and eaten and fucked and debauched.

sigh and sign and eye hungry pilgrim, if only you could have watched.

Francesca Can Too Stop Thinking about Sex, Reflect upon Her Position in Poetry, Write a Real Sonnet

pilgrim, i did not mean to be so loose
of tongue, so bold in all i loosely told
in my smut so smug, so overly sold.
i did not mean, pilgrim, to traduce.

i apologize, i offer no excuse:
but, poet, though you have right to scold
it was highsouled you who made my mouth hold
what it held and tell what it told. a truce,

no, let's call it an honor. mine is apt,
as far as long sentences go: my vice
in your verse will tempt others to try

and sing: readers, lovers forever rapt
and about to sweetly sigh: paradise!
thank you, poet, for keeping me alive.

Look at Lesbia Now!

and look at lesbia now! she's said farewell
to her face: dark-circled
nipples down and dark
she's even let the hair grow back down there.
right, she's not a real blonde, and
no one's knocking at her door anymore.
we all knew it would turn out like this.

o lesbia, daughter of ____ and wife of _____ and mistress of _____
mother of _____, ha! ceded what? the one so valued
what she had on her once pretty mind
she traded in everyone for that? did you hear
she wouldn't have a baby with her lover
even if he promised to keep it in a tent out back?
so he left.
have you seen her walking alone thru this black-and-white town
her pink ipod playing ryan adams, spoon, rilo kiley,
lucinda, arcade fire, the silver jews, mark mulcahy,
yeah, dylan; sufjan stevens, even,
wearing her usual yellow-pink-blue woolen cap?

let the kindergarten parents talk:
yeah, you know, the divorced one, the "poet",
the one who wears "the jeans",
bags under her pink eyes, her young boyfriend
just moved back to new york.

It Is to Have or Nothing

Of all the forms of being—

I like a table

And

I like a lake.

The excitement of an upandcoming

Mistake:

Do not send word to your lover

If you cannot decide which one.

Involvement, like war, is a form

Of divination. Think

About what you said—or didn't—

That's why it hurts to swallow.

My first words in French?

Cruche, olivier, fenêtre,

Et, peut-être,

Pilier, tour.

Yeah, for a while they were "involved"—

Then they "delved" into

"Abjure".

Uncertainty more exciting than sex!

We could do serious, but

My lover was NO FUN.

O creamy cloud, indecision, I love you. I love you. I love you.

So badly. So slowly

I want to enter you

From behind.

O ignorant protagonist

The lineaments of my face—

We had an interval,

A ludicrous,

"Us", the most fleeting

Of all.

I was

A tachiste, a revenant;

He a revanchist.

Yeah, what felt at what saw.

Listen: the next time you cry it won't be

At a train station

In France—you died at that scene—

To leave is to leave—

Well enough.

I am so—

Not lonely.

Worn and dark was my...

Bright blue my...

Sometimes you just wanna press Send, thinking

If this is what ends it all, so I am.

I will send you glück's purple bathing suit—

Even if it kills us.

That's how I tell the story—"We were involved for a while—long was

Our distance—and, mostly—wrong—finally

I sent him Louise Glück's 'Purple Bathing Suit'—

Never to hear from him again".

The train schedule was an étude.

Was I no longer eager

To study my lover?

In my lap coleridge's constancy to an ideal object.

In the end:

A newly cleared

Table.

And, if cleanly forgotten, a little lost

Lake.

SONNET (seized)

i want to be, monk,
unmade
unbecome
unfabricated:
unadulterated
unborn
undone

instead, announced my orgasm in this my songing
stopped short,

and thus began my longing...

My Lover Asks Me to Consider

but i don't know what. i can not see it.
what is he pointing to? what is he talking about? that tree
over there in old blooms dying, but refusing to not tree
up? the moon already fake and fading,

but still sexed, still hot? is it humility? sincerity? alacrity?
celerity? is it sin? is it love? love, is it doubt?
purity? humanity? maybe politics? um, literature?
well, then, poetry or fiction?
is it a lamp?
(at least i know it is not a pipe!)

milton, who declined every dualism,
doesn't know what he is saying!
harold bloom who understands everything is asking:
could it be the active and aggressive process of defense?
vico still bravely braying: we can only understand
what we ourselves have made (up!).

when you looked at me your eyes imprinted (imparted)
your grace in me and for this you loved me ardently
and thus my eyes deserved to adore what they beheld in you.

say what?
i say: *fuck!* and *fuck you!* and *come on!*

and *i love you!* and *shit!* and:

enough!

My Love Sent Me a List

O my Love sent me a lusty list,
Did not compare me to a summer's day
Wrote not the beauty of mine eyes
But catalogued in a pretty detailed
And comprehensive way the way(s)
In which he was better than me.
"More capable of extra- and inter-
Polation. More well-traveled -rounded multi-
Lingual! More practiced in so many matters
More: physical, artistic, musical,
Politic(al) academic (I dare say!) social
(In many ways!) and (ditto!) sexual!"
And yet these mores undid but his own plea(s)(e)
And left, none-the-less, the Greater Moor of me.

Fragmentary

this poem would if it could make you
feel like total shit
regret mixed with lilacs and way too many
cigarettes

You Are Who

i think i will not say anything for a while
i think i will not tell what i am thinking

i will just sit right here and check and count
how horny am i and how much money do i have at the moment

until i know something about something
ahead instead of behind all those other cities

what green and gold and how many marked corners
how we hated everyone except ourselves

everyone was awful but the sky
always kinda blue and nice above us

think of how you still love yourself best
how best you think what you are thinking

don't worry i won't write a poem about it
my sexual and poetic powers are waning

and you—you are showing signs of being older
than anything i have ever seen before

or at least anything that i knew so well
when we were young you are who i was

with this you

who is so wrong and so old
although of course i barely know this

Once the Beauty Abishag

Was once the beauty
Abishag, a witch of Grafton,
Coos—remember—
whatever you needed—
i had done for you—

truth thought was weak
beside that truth that didn't
look like truth at all:

in the sun on hands and knees
but my hair was dry—
and you grew strange and stronger—
poisoned—by which you surely meant
bewitched—so i would last you—longer—

ALLOVER POEM B(L)AM in this corner I was raped almost 3 years ago—brutally would not be accurate but would also not not be. that was just to the short side of way over (t)here, here, the year i lost my mind over losing my face: the eyes mostly, the way they were wrong: i ran miles and miles with them still in my head: they saw, they saw. no, no one else up here in the top of this poem which is really the middle of the life (unless, unless...). yeah, i did, even though lived my alone watching something sometimes would cry would want would want would want NOT-THIS would want to own and be owned. be care taken of. listened to drake. listened to kanye. listened to jay-z. could romanticize everyone's but me. BLAM. butt jolie. but butt jolie? robert irwin, why does your staring at a wall look and feel so much better than me staring at a wall? why do you look so good in my poem? i hear (read read) you run 8 miles a day and are very happy. or is it 5? i will (probably not) look it up in seeing is forgetting the name of the thing that you see up in my bedroom where the bed is the only thing left: so tempting, so sexy: listened to kanye. listened to jay-z. read us magazine. tolstoy. murakami. natasha and andrei? tengo and amomame? SHIT MOTHER FUCKER shit mother fucker just me on me on me: raised 2 kids: ALONE. ran 2,589 miles in 3 years: never once looked up to see. BANG BANG? discarded more people than i could possibly ever learn or know. was not there anyone that didn't grow fat and stale, thin and selfish, just plain fucking dumb? i had all the ideas here. here: a rimini blue on a rimini bird. here: a sheepskin on top of a chair. rearranged the living room. (lived the room. roomed the living.) here: alone, me. here i thought about you, i.e., just sat here, smelling my own pussy, ugly as fuck and yet so beautiful—you should have a photo of everytime. everyday: every me me me me me: my dark brow. my blonde hair: all that's best of shade and light: dirty. stringy. squeaky. clean. and underneath it all was all was nothing all muscle all self all i and you is

the biggest joke

in the canon: KA—BOOk after book after book. barely shook, barely trembled. un-like kierkegaard un-like rothko un-like rilke. un-roth un-larkin un-roethke. un-updike. un-kanye: all them big ni$$a boys. each of them should have been (with) me. but this poem has no little man in it,

and DOES NOT HAVE A SINGLE UNMOVING PART
and is full of fucking empty
productivity? was not ever able to make or be. so what can I do for you? here? and now? what do you want? did I forget to ask? fuck you. fuck you all over the bottom of this page, this poem. it's flesh-colored down here and complicated and dekooning pink and green and there is no room left is black and is blue and is layered over layer over mile over something over
somebody—moonlit? shit. just shut the fuck up.
i'm is done. and you and i is over. and not once, not
once did you think or care to ask: is there something small
i can possibly try/make/say/think? for you?

Least Said

Maybe we you us
But not everyone except
Everyone else seemingly set
One could romanticize the shipbells
Out of somebody else's grocery, sex shopping, life cleaning, bills
Of sail. When they had fresh grapefruit it was nothing like you not having
Scurvy, with or without the vodka. Your friends
Did they still say things (?) and the masses—
No, one didn't want to picture that vast
Writhing. Self-love is better left to this selective peculiar:
One shelf over, top shelf. The yeats, the years, none of it
More real than this. The judgment, the particular partings:
Reading a new yorker article about you. Reading. An article.
A small monster at my toe. There was once a long lusty list but
The only thing s/he had on me was feet. I went to course, to game, to
College. The epiphany was not worth dwelling (placement word of
Your choice here). Not to speak of, or the her, him, him before him, your last
Lover but, "seeing someone else right now"? Mostly, the possessive pronoun
"Her" in the next clause. Whose unfairness? Be-spoken and be-longing.
(An embarrassment of melons and heavily salted meats.)
The thing you will miss was being sexy, you will forget that you went
Forgetting all along; the whole ride. Going, going. Not coming. Reading.
Too closely, will fail my the measure of some treasure
You believe exists, but how? Morning was the only mooring: feeling,
Thinking, seeing no one. Right
Now. Or now. Barely tolerated, living.

Methow 19:19

i yearn for no one today
and i've no hope to one day
my children will come back
from california my x-husband will return and soon
i will fly to new york and see and not see all
my x-loves i will love none of them
i will have se-x with some of them
the songs are not about them
and never will be

help me, Horse, for i can neither neigh nor sigh
if Thou hast truly made me in Thy Sinewy Likeness:
Let Down the Coarse Ropes in Your Neck
the Yellow Gorsed Sleep in the Corner
of Your Wet Black Eye

Intempestive

Like this you went
through the warm stubble fields
indecent with the season
soft-lifted half-dead
out of sorts and reasons
moving through the sharp and stinging
new that smelled of what
had already happened
it was only sadness
in spring but it was melancholia
in autumn the temperate
current bringing back what
would never be or do
yet somehow sweeter
what the late breeze lifted
borrowed brought what
was already done
greener for its yellow
warmer for its sad
and colder its beforetaken
carrying the late baby
bald and sleeping
inside you in springtime
outside you in fall
you would have to wait
to stay to say spring was
a studied sadness compared
to this forced from the forest
like a hungry bird proleptic
leave-taking—adieu!—
never liked the stubble field
so much as now turning round
to see love undonefor already
dreaming "ghost"—adieu!—

sadder for its wind and end -lessness
this orchard and all the babies grown
more poignant grace winged and limbed
is it too late to witness
to bear what one did
manage to see and smell
and unknow almost almost
there soon soon
there will be nothing
less than nothing
left now it's still just
late still
to go still quick like a poppy
late and last in the soon
and sickening snow

Orpheus and Eurydice (2005)

that's how the hip souls went:
from brooklyn to manhattan
and back.

vibrant
in their lowkey finery
yet almost nondescript
dirtyhaired, flared, satchels full of hipster shit
(like what? dostoyevsky and parliaments?)
earbuds faintly blossoming some new deflowered sounds
they silently moved their blood
(much like our own lifeblood)
through arteries
through arteries hard as stone
silent thoughtful pale stoned? and almost
dead

that one lowslung skijacketed skinnyhipped girl's lips:

otherwise nothing else was red...

o the mind mind has mountains cliffs of fall
frightful sheer no man fathomed
hold them cheap may who ne'er hung there...

what are you doing here?

—who?

and it was so: on the way down
to the underground years and years ago
i had left him or, more accurately, will say some,
at broadway and lafayette, he had left me

for ne'er again, he had promised, her to see
but nine years later there i was again
having embarked on a randomly chosen F train
he watched her walk in

had he been riding back and forth
all these years? had he never gotten off?

her hair was loose i was blonder thinner older
than the tree he planted and remembered me by
wearing cowboy boots and a pink jacket,
a face, his human face

in front of mine: *what are you doing*
here? a question to which there were many but
no ready reply. he did not require. i rose.

(o rose tendrils strung in the limbs
of an olive tree) this was
the moment: him
and me.

had i been a form of blonde transcendence
and a hanging garden in his double bed?
he had been that thing you think
so hard and sharp upon before you let go and fall in

for all that, he must of said to himself, there she is.

he said: i hear a lot of you of late. me: how? you inquire?
his face full of face and eyes and strain.
(what hard mishap hath doomed this gentle swain?)
explain:

two roads he said diverged when last we spoke
and i, i supposedly took the one paved in con-
fessional poetry and sex, he the one
more steadandfaithandfruitful and less harried by.

what is, i said, the best approach?
protecting the ones we love
or exposing some/our truth? each
in its stubborn way beyond reproach.

(perhaps he only meant his lyre grew from his right
shoulder, mine from my left. it was april after all,
mixing memory and desire,
after all, it was the national month.)

for many years that backward glance was my way of life of art
i was made by that being apart
being denied fullfilled me beyond fullfillment.
i kept looking there: from many vantages,
i just closed my eyes, and he was there:

remember, he came up to me.
he could of rode that train and disappeared
silently, with just a new pink-eyed and corduroyed vision of me yet,
he chose to speak to his apparition

for all that, he must of said to himself, she is there.

he had watched me walk in!
what must have fluttered behind his eyes, inside
his neck and heart and hands
and cock. what would he do or say?
speak to her or let her form form a new image

from which to once again fade away? decay.
how long did he take to decide? one stop.

he asked about my new lover
i shook my head in bold reply
as if 'twas true: new lovers we should never try

who was behind who? and who afraid... of what?
and who afraid of looking where? back? was it back?

which way was the train headed on its track?
o whose fingers on whose lyre?

like elizabeth bishop and robert lowell
but less and callower and worse
yet who would prove the stouter soul?
who would come back whole from below?

we agreed: it would have been harder five years ago
i'm over you i said, but maybe it wasn't true
i said: usually i look way better than this. if i had known i would have tried...
perhaps that too was pansy freaked with jet, a lie.

o who was the poet and who is the muse? and what is/was the use... *it nothing skills... what boots it...*
what recks it them... what need they... they are sped
i would go up and use it, of course, but
a single backlook would be the ruin of his life, his
work: so near perfection: he stood:

i gotta go, and i: that's it?
he was the one to first ascend into the upper air
where all the love-dead live and breathe:
23rd street. he floated up and that was that. was it.

i did not turn to watch him go.
the doors (shiny exit gates?) must have opened and then
they must have simply closed.
on 57th i stopped and bought new shoes.
then i called my latest lover to report the latest news.

and while having phone sex—
these sad last few numbers rang:

o, i dreamt a long-lasting dream, years
it held fast to my small teeming brain,
but now 'tis lightly loosened from my fair-haired head—
i weep for matthew rohrer—he is dead.

Procession

I had just read *Auroras of Autumn*,
and *Brazil, January 1, 1502*,
and was reading *Clepsydra* when,
in the of corner of my left eye, in the left corner of the front window
broken earlier this winter and still not fixed, a hearse went by.
Odd, unheard of, down this little street
that lets out on one end only.
My heart was beating oddly as I had just opened the mail.
It took a while to understand that it was happening
now. That there were cars behind it and they were headed to some one
exact and extant spot. By the time I got there
a lady was drinking from a mug something that must be
cold by now. The cup was white. As was the only car
I could identify for it plainly read: *Camaro* under, yes,
a racing stripe. The friends and family were Native. A young girl
adjusted her topknot in that little mirror the passenger is allowed to use
if she should so choose; then someone was passing something to someone
in the back. They took it and shook it over their up-cupped palm: maybe candy
that turns into gum. Everyone's hair was black. Only one woman
wore dark glasses, as I would have done. The sky
was dirty. The cars were dirty, the road was solid dirty
snow and ice. Suddenly, there was not one after the last one.

Clearer Brighter Lighted Now

what happened in the dark
which craftsman's touch
on one last necessary scene:

turns out: the devil's big, but doesn't even have
a ____. or it doesn't work.
what is ruined is HIS life.

fit the fair
long-haired luminous
angels (!) numerous and rare: gossiping stepping
back and forth
over the threshold. yay! almost living pink and breathing blue
from the greengrey posthumous garden
(from the hues and humors of the evening)
into this house, this verse, my lusty life
and i, long-haired luminous, will not be fooled nor stopped:

this is mine.
i'm that one, there: so golden grey:
as lovely of face as any corner of that ceiling
and with the thighs of HIS last judgment deciding who
can stay (the innocent shall be taken in, welcomed
by the learned and lo!—old
at least, as lean and learning lovers) who
can stay blazoning can stay proclaiming
who will stay the doom
and motherfuck! who damned and who—
o star-spangled sky—gone forever

Neither Snow Shovel nor Hoe

There was absolutely no way
to make a life, no matter how much you read,
how much time alone.

A very nice man,
veritably “strapping” and “you know what that’s for”
I booted up, “got
my stagger back” was suddenly happy thinking
about a possible walk after dark, whence I would not be raped and could
show off a mountain, like it was fucking
mine.

One day he “want to know everything about you”
he “like you even more after seeing you with your kids”
died unawares when given the opportunity
to follow up on why I felt
“kinda saddish and weird”.

Yes, I hear you,
why do I always secretly refer to things?
Things almost no one will know?

Some one is knocking, they have taken a shower,
put on a fancy corduroy shirt and come to tell you
they have googled you
you are beautiful
“I must now pack
and go”.

Lyana Sick and Next to Her

lyana sick and next to her i lay
as if myself in fever fretted head
and thought on him that i recorded dead

as if laudanum as if claret
as if it weren't over yet

brought him to mind again and again
beseeching him like thought to stay
then move do something that i could and did not will
live a little while i held him there

but again and again he overclouded disappeared
(he lives aftermiles and afteryears away from here)
i had to keep incanting him from scratch

i loved him once or didn't
get a chance so resurrected him as i lay
with my sick child and dear small she
stroked my hot and poisoned head

the dream went on all afternoon
so glad was i with hcr alone to dwell
in that sick and sunny afterroom
where we would aftertime be well

My Geranium

In my kitchen
on the windowsill
in a chipped green bowl
                    (with flourishes of gilt-edged white)
is the world's best geranium
she's the tallest the most beautiful of all

so gold

right now in her prime
flowering spreading and just begun
palms up! palms up!
she proudly begged and bedded the sun

A small crystal ball
(it wouldn't hang from the chandelier at all)
lies beneath her in her dirt
kaleidoscopic

she has a view of the mountains

Her stems have fast surpassed
the man-made stuck-in

furled note-flag on a thin wooden stick:
"you must be patient for a little while"
and the metal cake-tester even thinner
with the head of a broken plastic fox

his mouth turned round
his face in two directions—

nothing baking, janus

My geranium is better than all of summer
she does not need a new lover, yet

there is nothing yellow about her
she's thinking about death

Fragmentary

this poem takes place in the
is the cemetery
is the
statuary

is depicted as moonlit, is white, is absent
is present
is dependent on light on moon

is the speaker
is addressing and is pleading

yes, this,

again,

Show Up

at dawn i will rise
to mow my lawn
like the fine young widower
i am

but at dusk i lie still
in the muskeg of my lust
my *i need i want i*
must

and some sometimes one
time time and again lover
busy taken by at
my side

just one time, lover
take me as for what
i am

a not so sleepy not so dreamy
an unreasonable an unseasonable
beauty night can no longer
make right

but my god, what you can awaken to
slaken to rain after so much
sun or vice
verse

each mow row

a year in

a past

a lost

a crossed

a frost covered

a last life

alas life

intact families are all alike
getting into their cars
in raincoats that shine yellow
navy red

thank your dandelion stars
no one is yet is already
dead

lovers, do not come to me
in the dark arrive in the unreal
sidelight of the sidereal
day

pull back your tree covered
curtains to what this world did is
doing while you were down
gone

alas life

at last life

under the nimble limbo of the nimbo
stratus and sphere
right here

in the short torn negligee of my self
-neglect -respect and my wreaking
gore-tex sneakers

i will have finally shorn
all my scorn then some
fine morn let the line
form:

let all my loves and lovers have the courage to show up
show me what i was worth on this shooting sky green earth

Hello Poem

Aren't you supposed to be all alive and tell me what is going on? What is
A-happening?
Poem, why so nonplussed? So hors-rendu? So hasard? So misérable?
Poem, you are supposed to be for me
Not against me.
Do not tell me that part of the problem is I know I am hot!
It's spring, Poem, take us outside.
Poem, why did I come home from France without any idée and an Italian
Vogue?
Poem—so silent so—handsome, Poem.
So Mediterranean.
Poem, you have a nice face,
A good form, but
Poem—you are wrongheaded.
Poem—I want to be left alone.
Such a dabbler you are, Poem—a dilettante
And a Renaissance man.
So hard to tell, Poem, till you take off your clothes.
Poem, I think you are straight.
Poem, I know Hemingway baise-ed you in the derrière.
Poem, I know you are freer from history than prose fiction or drama!
Poem—do you want to be translated into French?
Poem—avez-vous ce que vous voulez?
French poem, you are very sexy.
Poem—did you depart for Marseille?
Poem—votre train is retarded! Quelle voie? Quelle garde?
Dream poem, you have shaved genitals!
Poem you are a plump pretty girl with feather earrings and a quick thick
Unread book.
Poem, eat my poussez!
Poem, Kay Ryan doesn't like you!
Not at all!
Poem you have an engraved stone for a heart!
(No, I will not tell you with what.)

A sheep for a lover.
Poem, you farted in your sleep.
Poem, you only have to do it once...
Poem, you get so sad at all the right/wrong places.
Poem, I'm afraid your strangeness is still not that true.
O Poem, we could have been so good together!
Poem, you think you are working, but
Poem—get a job.
Poem—get a life.
(Then, of course,
You of all people
Poem, must
Change it.)

Poem—you say too little.
Poem—you are so not enough.

SONNET (full-court press)

having studied swarthmore charts and mirrors,
fashion magazines, foucault, bloom, bad light,
whereof—hereof—had not become clearer;
what vision to present as first self-sight.

self quit; put on boots and a see-through dress.
some thought it was ironic "self-object-
ification", said they were not impressed.
some guessed that "honesty" was self's subject,

were put off nonetheless. self-asked: to sleep
with me? who would? self flat, self one inch deep.
self-glimpsed not much in that giant mirror:
innocence -credulity, self doth protest!

hey! presumptuous interlocutor!
pissed off, thwarted, played, and soon, undressed!

Threshold

what i should of softly sweetly surely said:
“o wingèd boy, come read with me in bed”.

Note(s)

A lot of this stuff was stolen from a lot of other stuff—with respect and apologies.

About the Author

Olena Kalytiak Davis “lives” in Anchorage, Alaska.

Lannan Literary Selections

For two decades Lannan Foundation has supported the publication and distribution of exceptional literary works. Copper Canyon Press gratefully acknowledges their support.

LANNAN LITERARY SELECTIONS 2014

Mark Bibbins, *They Don't Kill You Because They're Hungry, They Kill You Because They're Full*

Malachi Black, *Storm Toward Morning*

Marianne Boruch, *Cadaver, Speak*

Jericho Brown, *The New Testament*

Olena Kalytiak Davis, *The Poem She Didn't Write and Other Poems*

RECENT LANNAN LITERARY SELECTIONS FROM COPPER CANYON PRESS

James Arthur, *Charms Against Lightning*

Natalie Diaz, *When My Brother Was an Aztec*

Matthew Dickman and Michael Dickman, *50 American Plays*

Michael Dickman, *Flies*

Kerry James Evans, *Bangalore*

Tung-Hui Hu, *Greenhouses, Lighthouses*

Laura Kasischke, *Space, in Chains*

Deborah Landau, *The Last Usable Hour*

Sarah Lindsay, *Debt to the Bone-Eating Snotflower*

Michael McGriff, *Home Burial*

Valzhyna Mort, *Collected Body*

Lisa Olstein, *Little Stranger*

Roger Reeves, *King Me*

Ed Skoog, *Rough Day*

John Taggart, *Is Music: Selected Poems*

Jean Valentine, *Break the Glass*

Dean Young, *Fall Higher*

For a complete list of Lannan Literary Selections from Copper Canyon Press, please visit Partners on our website: www.coppercanyonpress.org

Poetry is vital to language and living. Since 1972, Copper Canyon Press has published extraordinary poetry from around the world to engage the imaginations and intellects of readers, writers, booksellers, librarians, teachers, students, and donors.

WE ARE GRATEFUL FOR THE MAJOR SUPPORT PROVIDED BY:

THE PAUL G. ALLEN FAMILY FOUNDATION

amazon.com

Lannan

THE MAURER FAMILY FOUNDATION

Anonymous

John Branch

Diana Broze

Beroz Ferrell & The Point, LLC

Janet and Les Cox

Mimi Gardner Gates

Gull Industries, Inc.
on behalf of William and Ruth True

Linda Gerrard and Walter Parsons

Mark Hamilton and Suzie Rapp

Carolyn and Robert Hedin

Steven Myron Holl

Lakeside Industries, Inc.
on behalf of Jeanne Marie Lee

Maureen Lee and Mark Busto

Brice Marden

Ellie Mathews and Carl Youngmann as The North Press

H. Stewart Parker

Penny and Jerry Peabody

John Phillips and Anne O'Donnell

Joseph C. Roberts

Cynthia Lovelace Sears and Frank Buxton

The Seattle Foundation

Dan Waggoner

Charles and Barbara Wright

The dedicated interns and faithful volunteers of Copper Canyon Press

TO LEARN MORE ABOUT UNDERWRITING COPPER CANYON PRESS TITLES, PLEASE CALL 360-385-4925 EXT. 103

The Chinese character for poetry is made up of two parts:
"word" and "temple." It also serves as pressmark for
Copper Canyon Press.

The poems are set in Sabon.
Book design and composition by Phil Kovacevich.